Riding Out

ALSO BY INGRID KLIMKE

Cavalletti
Basic Training of the Young Horse
Training Horses the Ingrid Klimke Way

INGRID KLIMKE

—Riding Out

Strategies for Training Outside the Arena to Improve Horse Health and Performance

Translated by Helen McKinnon

Trafalgar Square
North Pomfret, Vermont

First published in the United States of America in 2024 by
Trafalgar Square Books, North Pomfret, Vermont

Originally published in German as *Reiten im Gelände: Sicheres Ausreiten, Konditionstraining, Kleine Geländehindernisse*.

Copyright © 2023 Ingrid Klimke and Franckh-Kosmos Verglas-GmbH & Co. KG
English translation © 2024 Trafalgar Square Books

All rights reserved. No part of this book may be reproduced, by any means, without written permission of the publisher, except by a reviewer quoting brief excerpts for a review in a magazine, newspaper, or website.

Disclaimer of Liability
The author and publisher shall have neither liability nor responsibility to any person or entity with respect to any loss or damage caused or alleged to be caused directly or indirectly by the information contained in this book. While the book is as accurate as the author can make it, there may be errors, omissions, and inaccuracies.

Trafalgar Square Books encourages the use of approved safety helmets in all equestrian sports and activities.

Trafalgar Square Books certifies that the content in this book was generated by a human expert on the subject, and the content was edited, fact-checked, and proofread by human publishing specialists with a lifetime of equestrian knowledge. TSB does not publish books generated by artificial intelligence (AI).

ISBN: 978-1-64601-221-3
Library of Congress Control Number: 2024931670

Text: Ingrid Klimke, Alexandra Haungs
German Editor: Alexandra Haungs
Design Concept: Peter Schmidt Group GmbH, Hamburg
Interior Design: Atelier Krohmer, Dettingen/Erms
Cover Design: RM Didier
Production: Claudia Frank
Photography: All photographs by Horst Streitferdt/KOSMOS, except p. 58, p. 65 top, p. 66 upper right by Jens Feierabend/jfx pictures.

Printed in the United States of America

10 9 8 7 6 5 4 3 2 1

Contents

1 INTRODUCTION—
  The Great Outdoors

3 EXPLORING THE OUTDOORS—
  on Horseback

4 **Why I Love Trail Riding**
4 Variety for Dressage Horses
5 Varied Basic Training for Young Horses
6 Getting Used to Environmental Stimuli
6 Sure-Footedness
7 Building Strength and Fitness
7 What the Rider Learns
7 Riding Year-Round, in Any Weather

11 READY FOR THE TRAIL—
   Ride and Relax

12 **Out-of-the-Arena Basics**
12 Equipment for the Rider
13 Equipment for the Horse
14 Never Ride Out Alone

15 **Riding in a Group**
15 Putting a Group Together
19 Be Considerate
19 Keep a Distance
19 Warm-Up

20 The Rider's Seat and Aids
20 Footing Conditions
21 Speed
22 Slowing Down with Control
23 Riding Away from the Group
24 Voltes or Large Circles
25 Turn-on-the-Forehand
25 Changing the Lead Rider
25 Riding on the Road
26 Crossing Roads

27 **Safety First**

33 WATER CROSSINGS—
   A Refreshing Activity

34 **Getting Used to Water**
34 An Essential Exercise
34 Start with a Lead Horse
36 Walk, Then Trot, Then Canter

43 JUMPING OBSTACLES—
   Outside the Arena

44 **Preparing for Jumping**
44 Always Begin in Walk
46 Warm Up in Rising Trot
46 Preparatory Canter Work
48 Control and Stopping
48 Summary

49 Position and Plan
49 Basic Rules
51 Summary
52 The Chris Bartle "Oh, Crap!" Seat
52 Rider Requirements

53 Cross-Country Obstacles
53 Rolling Track
54 Logs
56 Brush Fences
57 Ditches
59 Summary
60 Steps and Banks
62 Summary

68 Jumping Into and Out of Water
69 Preparation
70 What to Do
70 What Can Happen?

75 FITNESS TRAINING— Outside the Arena

76 Fitness, Strength, and Building Muscle
76 Start Slowly
77 Riding Up and Down Hills
79 Working on Hills
80 Canter Work
82 Interval Training

87 SUPPLING— Outside the Arena

88 Dressage Out on the Trail
88 Benefits
89 Exercises Out on the Trail

90 Lengthened Strides
90 Lengthened Strides in Trot
92 Lengthened Strides in Canter

94 Flying Changes
95 Working on Flying Changes
96 Flying Changes Out on the Trail
97 Know When to Stop

101 LAST BUT NOT LEAST
103 Recommended Reading

INTRODUCTION: THE GREAT OUTDOORS

Anyone who knows me knows I love riding outside. I enjoy riding out in the fresh air year-round, whatever the weather. For my horses and me, riding outside the arena is about enjoying life. It adds welcome variety to our everyday training, provides active relaxation, boosts motivation, and builds fitness.

As a child, I loved our Sunday family rides. You should expect the unexpected out on the trail, so these rides were often hair-raising. I found them exciting. My father insisted that we all ride out together on a Sunday. He called the rides "cavorting in the countryside," and all his dressage horses benefitted from them. It was something he passed onto me. On weekends when we weren't competing, we sometimes took up to 10 horses on our beloved Sunday rides. It's a day when family, team, and friends can relax and have fun. The most important thing about riding in the countryside is to enjoy it.

Riding outside the arena isn't just fun; it also provides horses with varied training. The things my horses learn out on the trail benefit me between the dressage boards and in the show jumping arena. Trail riding is an integral part of my event horses' training program. It's a topic close to my heart, and I'd like to share it with you in this book. I hope to be able to inspire you to enjoy "riding out."

You'll learn all about the right equipment; the ideal group formation; how to stay safe out on the trail; how to get your horse used to riding through water; how to jump small obstacles; and how to improve your horses' fitness, stamina, and strength. The last chapter is especially important to me because I advocate regularly riding dressage horses out on the trail. You'll find ideas for making use of the energy and fresh air of the open country. You'll discover suppling exercises to improve your dressage horse's motivation and fitness for the arena, and to help him develop a calm and unflappable frame of mind.

I hope you enjoy this book, and that you feel safe and have fun trail riding and conquering the great outdoors with your horse.

Ingrid Klimke

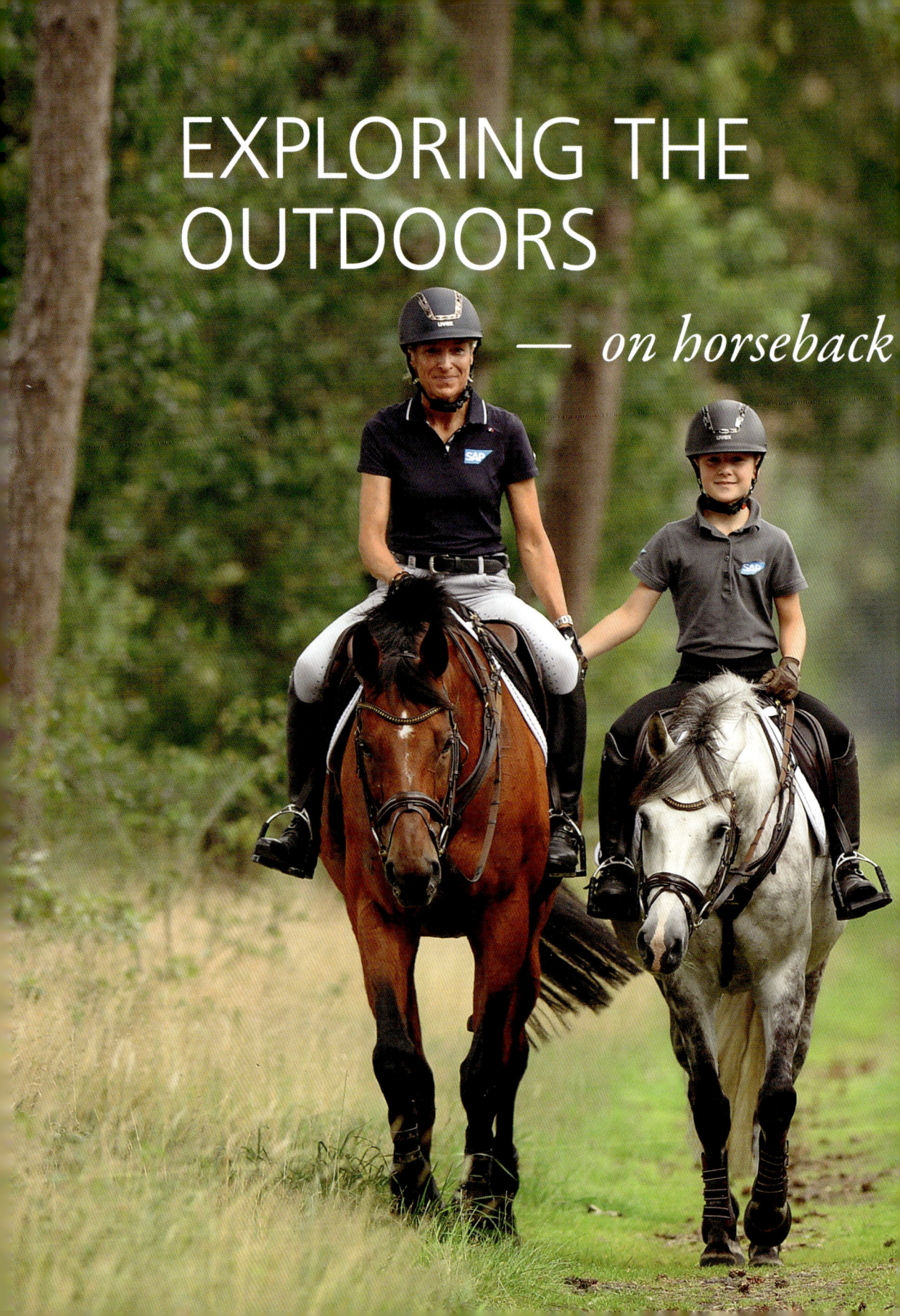

WHY I LOVE TRAIL RIDING

Nothing makes me happier than going out for a ride. It's a chance to enjoy the beautiful countryside, breathe in the fresh air, and forget about my worries for a while. For me, trail riding is active time out with my horses, and we deliberately make it part of our everyday life. There's nothing quite like trail riding for satisfying horses' innate desire for movement. Traveling through the countryside in a group is the most natural thing in the world for horses.

Trail riding also adds variety to their training plan, which boosts their motivation. That's why I take all my horses, including my dressage horses and youngsters, out on the trail.

VARIETY FOR DRESSAGE HORSES

All horses need variety, and their brains need a break. All my horses, including my dressage horses, enjoy varied training. They gain important experience outside the dressage arena. We practice dressage exercises when we're out riding, on hills, or in fields full of winter stubble. Work on slopes improves stamina and strengthens the muscles, especially in the hindquarters and back. The different sights and experiences out on the trail help make my horses calmer and more balanced. They learn to work independently and react quickly. I can tell from their calm, motivated outlook that this kind of training benefits them.

Whether you go for a nice, relaxing ride, or do some suppling work on hills, your horse will thank you, and his new-found strength and energy will help him shine in the dressage arena.

Trail riding is best in a group.

All our horses enjoy trail riding: eventing superstars Bobby and Scrabble, dressage horse Firlefranz, and Mustang the pony.

VARIED BASIC TRAINING FOR YOUNG HORSES

Training for young horses should be as varied as possible. The different types of ground you encounter on a trail ride have an important role to play. Some horses need to learn sure-footedness, for one. And for all horses, the more freedom outside they have when growing up and the more often they're exercised on different types of footing, the more balanced and sure-footed they will be.

Experience has shown me that trail riding is always beneficial, no matter what direction the rest of the horse's training takes. Varied basic training is extremely beneficial, especially if you plan to later specialize in dressage and jumping, disciplines that essentially depend on the horse's disposition. My book *Basic Training of the Young Horse* takes a detailed look at all the important aspects of training a young horse

The position of their ears shows that both mares are interested in what's going on around them.

GETTING USED TO ENVIRONMENTAL STIMULI

It's important for every horse to get used to different environmental stimuli. Trail riding exposes horses to lots of different conditions, which makes them more resilient. Whether it's the weather with its wind and rain, or unfamiliar objects such as flapping tarpaulins and passing tractors, or sudden noises or movements, or the wildlife you can encounter in the countryside—experiencing all these things helps make horses bolder and more unflappable. And the confidence they develop helps me, when I take them to a competition and they have to leave the familiar surroundings of home.

SURE-FOOTEDNESS

Trail riding trains the horse's whole body, including his natural reflexes. It helps develop nimbleness and sure-footedness and is the best way to get horses used to different footing conditions. Almost any surface—grass, sand, or forestry tracks, uphill or downhill—is suitable, depending on the weather conditions. When training, it's a good idea to do long periods of walk and short stretches of trot on firmer ground to strengthen the horse's tendons and ligaments. This doesn't just apply to eventers.

BUILDING STRENGTH AND FITNESS

The varied movement stimuli of a trail ride help to develop strength, stamina, and speed. Stretches of trot and canter improve horses' fitness on longer rides. Working on hills is particularly effective, strengthens the whole musculature, and helps improve suppleness. I also do regular work on hills with my dressage horses. You can read more about this starting on page 87 in the chapter "Suppling."

WHAT THE RIDER LEARNS

Trail riding doesn't just teach horses to be more relaxed and nimbler, and to develop stamina. Riders also gain valuable experience out in the countryside. You will get to know your horse better and learn to predict his reactions. Tackling new situations together helps mutual trust grow, too.

Trail riding makes the rider's seat more secure and balanced, and the experience the rider gains will help her confidence grow.

RIDING YEAR-ROUND, IN ANY WEATHER

I ride out year-round, in almost any weather. I find that every season is special in its own way. Many people think that spring is the best time of year for trail riding. You can see nature coming alive, the trees and bushes are coming into leaf, it isn't too hot, there aren't any flies, and the horses feel fresh and keen.

Summer is a great time of year for playing in the water, and hot weather often tempts us into the cool shade of the woods. The days are long, and we can go out for a ride early in the morning or later in the evening.

I love riding in stubble fields during late summer and autumn, and fox hunting now and then. I'm especially fond of the stillness of a misty November morning. My horse and I both enjoy the tranquility of nature.

I always hope to be able to ride out in snow in winter, but that doesn't happen in Münster, Germany, where I live, very often. Be aware that if horses have shoes on, snow can ball up in their hooves and they end up walking on stilts. It can help to use snow pads.

"For me, trail riding is about leaving my worries behind."

VARIETY YEAR-ROUND

Spring: A May ride past glorious rhododendron flowers in the park.

Summer: Forests and meadows are a tempting place to take off the brakes in canter.

November mist: Veteran Braxxi enjoyed ponying with us well into old age.

Photo Feature — Variety Year-Round

Winter wonderland: Freudentänzer investigates the powdery snow.

OUT-OF-THE-ARENA BASICS

EQUIPMENT FOR THE RIDER

Equipment is an important aspect of trail riding. This section of the book covers the equipment you and your horse will need. Let's start at the top. Helmets are obviously always important. Never ride without a helmet! Sometimes I wear a back protector; sometimes I don't. If you feel safer with a back protector, then wear one, but you don't have to. However, if you're planning to do any jumping, then a back protector is essential. You should wear gloves and carry a whip to back up your leg if you need to. Small, blunt, rounded spurs can be helpful for supporting the forward aids in an emergency. A high visibility vest ensures that you can be seen when riding in the dark or during winter.

A breastplate with an integrated neck strap is part of my standard equipment.

With the right equipment, horse and rider can safely enjoy riding outside the arena.

EQUIPMENT FOR THE HORSE

The horse should wear whichever bit he normally wears for everyday training. Then, there is the breastplate, with an integrated neck strap the rider can grab in an emergency. Safety stirrups are also important to prevent your foot from getting caught in the event of a fall. The horse should wear splint boots or brushing boots, and if he tends to overreach, bell boots. Depending on the footing conditions, it may make sense to have studs added to your horse's shoes. Wet grass can be very slippery.

Fly spray is important in summer. Horses attract flies and biting insects, especially when they sweat. This causes horses unnecessary stress; they may struggle to concentrate or even become unwilling. This isn't just annoying when you are out for a ride—it can also be dangerous. Make sure you always spray your horse with plenty of fly spray before you set off. A fly bonnet will keep annoying flies away from your horse's ears, too.

If you ride in winter or when it's getting dark at night, it's important for your horse to wear reflective boots or wraps, a reflective quarter sheet, or even a light-up neck strap for visibility.

Check your horse's equipment thoroughly before setting off. Are the saddle and bridle sitting correctly and are all leather straps in good condition? Then all you need to do is check your girth, shorten your stirrups, and you are ready to go.

Never alone: riding in pairs is safer than riding alone.

NEVER RIDE OUT ALONE

It's time to head out and enjoy the trail. But there are a few things you should keep in mind. The most important rule is: never ride out alone.

It's good to begin by riding out in a small group. Two is the ideal number, since each of you only has one other horse and rider to look out for. Experienced, steady horses can be ridden in walk on a loose rein at the beginning of the ride. Inexperienced riders should ride with the longest rein possible while still maintaining contact with the horse's mouth, because you never know what might happen.

Experienced riders can make "green" riders feel more secure by leading her, especially in the beginning. Use a lead rope with a snap that can't open by mistake, and make sure the rope is long enough that it doesn't pull the horses into each other, but not so long that it drags on the ground when the horses are a safe distance apart. Inexperienced riders can also be led in trot. This allows everyone to be safer and stay in control.

Trail riding differs from riding in an indoor or outdoor arena in a few ways. As herd animals, horses feel happiest in a group of their own species, so they enjoy going out with other horses. Horses usually go forward willingly in company.

Most horses are more alert in natural surroundings and can sometimes even be a little anxious, so the rider should be prepared for sudden spooks.

> **PREREQUISITES**
> — The horse should have a solid foundation.
> — The rider should have basic skills.
> — The horse and rider should be compatible.
> — The rider should be aware of the special demands of trail riding.
> — The ride should be well planned.

RIDING IN A GROUP

You should think carefully about the composition of your riding group before setting off on a trail ride together. Always think about who will be safe in which position in the group. Let me explain.

PUTTING A GROUP TOGETHER

Having an experienced horse-and-rider pair in the group is essential. An unflappable lead horse will help keep the rest of the group calm. This is especially important for potentially difficult situations, such as crossing roads, riding past unfamiliar objects, or riding through water. The experienced pair can be counted on to support other horses and riders.

Nervous riders should only ride out on confident and experienced trail horses. The anxious rider will learn to rely on her steady partner, the horse, and gradually become more confident. Even a nervous rider can lead a group on an experienced horse. Experienced riders need to be proactive and give their horses, whether green or with some mileage, a feeling of security in unfamiliar environments.

The two experienced horses lead this group.

READY FOR THE TRAIL — OUT-OF-THE-ARENA BASICS

When an experienced horse gives a safe experience, even a young rider can take the lead.

The experienced rider on a young, inexperienced horse can bring up the rear in the trail riding group. The young horse can take guidance from the other horses in front of him. The experienced rider can also keep an eye on the group ahead of her and hold them together.

Being in the middle of a group will help a less experienced rider control her horse. A rider at this level should be behind a good horse that won't kick if she brings her horse too close.

riders, if the ponies happen to run forward or if the kids lose control, which is why we need them behind two safe horses that don't kick. And then, at the back of our group, we have the horses that kick—these horses should never be in the middle.

When deciding who is safe in which position, first, you need to remember stallions should obviously never go behind mares. You should also keep in mind that dominant horses often prefer to lead. If there are dominant horses in my group, we tend to let them go in their preferred place, so they don't end up overtaking the other horses from behind because they really want to be in front.

We change the order within our group every now and then, as long as it's safe to do so. When younger and less experienced riders can control their horses safely within the group, they're ready to try taking the lead. They need to learn to ride their horses forward independently, and to steer and control them. This works best in a group that includes calm and experienced horses.

For example, with my group, if our ride is going well with the young riders and their ponies in the middle of the group, then it's time to get them used to the idea that they will sometimes go in front.

When our horses are as relaxed, we prefer to ride on the longest rein possible, so the rider can still stay in control if worst comes to worst, but the horse can relax and move freely. You can see how both horses and

When it comes to trail riding, safety should always come first.

When I go out on a trail ride with a group, we often have two good mares in front who will go past anything, and just as importantly, don't kick. Behind them, we usually have younger riders on their ponies. They might still end up too close to other

CONSIDER LESS EXPERIENCED HORSES AND RIDERS

When riding in a group, it's important to consider the less experienced members. Adapt the pace, speed, and difficulty of the ride to the least experienced horse and rider there.

riders can relax and enjoy riding out in a group. But now it's time for the ponies to be brave and trot forward, while the two experienced mares who usually lead prove themselves in the middle.

The rider at the back has the important job of ensuring the group stays together and making sure everyone is safe. If somebody falls off her horse, the group must stop as quickly as possible; if a rider is getting left behind, the rest of the group should reduce speed accordingly. Another rider from the group might also need to go back to help somebody else.

Practice riding and ponying another horse at the same time, in case someday a rider on a trail ride is injured and can't ride home independently, or in case somebody feels unsafe and wants to be led.

Do not overtake the lead rider. If a rider can't keep her horse at a safe distance and isn't able to circle back to create more space, she must call out to the lead rider to let her know she is going to overtake her.

If you have permission from a landowner to ride in fields instead of on an established trail, ride alongside each other to avoid wearing a track into the ground. You can spread out in a line or ride in a staggered formation

The riders at the back keep the group together and make sure they stay a safe distance from each other.

BE CONSIDERATE

It's important to show consideration to pedestrians and cyclists. The lead rider should alert other riders to their presence in plenty of time, with hand signals or a vocal call. If you don't have space to ride past cyclists or pedestrians in a wide arc, your group should travel by them at a walk. You should only start trotting or cantering when you are an appropriate distance away. The lead rider can also relay other important information with her voice or through hand signals—if there is a need to change pace, for example, or to alert other riders to hazards such as barbed wire or holes. Riders in the back of the group should immediately let riders in front of them know if somebody has fallen off or has been left behind. Staying within line of sight of others is essential.

TIPS FOR BEING CONSIDERATE

Pedestrians
Be friendly and pass in walk.

Farm Machinery
When haying or harvest work is taking place, avoid related machinery.

Forestry Logging
Give a wide berth.

Hunting
Avoid the edges of woodlands and wildlife observation hides at dawn and dusk. Wear safety orange.

Conservation and Environmental Considerations
Be aware of protected areas and respect signage.

Everyone should practice riding in front.

KEEP A DISTANCE

The ideal distance between riders is usually around two horse lengths. If the distance is too much bigger than that, horses in the back often want to catch up and be closer to the rest of the group. On the other hand, if the horses end up too close to each other, there's always the risk that the horse in front will kick. A distance of two horse lengths has worked quite well for my group in practice. The rider at the back has an important job. She needs to keep the group together and, if necessary, shout to the lead rider if something goes wrong in the middle of the group.

WARM-UP

When you go out for a ride, treat your horse and his muscles, tendons, and joints to an adequate warm-up. Ride at walk for at least 15 minutes before moving up into trot. When the group has warmed up, you can trot on.

The rider should have a secure contact on the reins, her weight should be in her heels, and she should have her eyes forward. This enables the rider to ride as effectively as possible.

THE RIDER'S SEAT AND AIDS

When you ride out through open fields or on a trail, your stirrups should always be two to four holes shorter than when you are riding in an indoor or outdoor arena. You should always post the trot to take strain off yourself and the horse's back. Remember to change diagonal at regular intervals to keep the load on each diagonal pair of legs as even as possible. Canter in a forward seat; this also takes strain off the horse's back and off the rider. You should make sure the horse does equal amounts of canter on the left and right lead, to avoid putting too much strain on either foreleg. If the horse doesn't strike off on the leg you wanted, or if he changes lead after just a few strides, come back to trot and try the transition again. If you and your horse are comfortable with flying changes, then you can use them instead.

FOOTING CONDITIONS

The condition of the footing on your ride is always important to consider, for the sake of

READY FOR THE TRAIL — OUT-OF-THE-ARENA BASICS

the horse's health. The ground should be soft and springy, and neither too wet nor too deep; this is especially important for cantering at a faster pace. Dry grass and sandy surfaces are ideal. The footing can also change, depending on the weather. Sandy soil can become heavy after a prolonged spell of dry weather or rain. Grass can become very heavy or slippery after rain, or hard after a dry spell.

It's best to avoid riding in deep tracks, whether from animals or machinery. And note that unshod horses often go better on stony or gravelly ground if they are wearing hoof boots. Avoid cantering on stony or gravelly surfaces.

If you want to canter, do it on a level stretch or a slight incline where you can clearly see the ground ahead of you.

SPEED

It's important that the rider always maintain a secure contact with the horse's mouth; the reins shouldn't be too loose, and the rider should be able to set a controlled pace. The pace shouldn't be too free but rather well-regulated. After loosening up in trot (following your walk warm-up), you can go into a brisk working trot, depending on the composition of the group and the temperament of the horses. After the trot phase, you can move into your first steady canter.

Later in the ride, you can try increasing the pace of the canter over shorter distances. High energy horses enjoy having the chance to burn off energy in canter. However, the horse should always be under control so you can stop if you need to.

> **"LONG REIN" AND "LOOSE REIN"**
>
> A "long rein" means you allow the horse as much freedom in his neck as he needs to stretch into the hand, but you maintain a light contact with the horse's mouth. A "loose rein" means holding the reins by the buckle; there is no contact between the rider's hand and the horse's mouth.

Make sure you allow the horse to relax by including extended breaks in walk, after trotting and especially after cantering. This will give you and your horse a breather and prevent you from asking too much of him. The horse's pulse and respiratory rate will settle.

As a general rule, every period of exertion should be followed by a quiet, easy wander in walk that not only helps the horse relax physically but also helps balance his mental equilibrium. If your horse is calm and relaxed, ride at walk on a long rein, maintaining a light contact with the horse's mouth. You can give your horse a loose rein if he is calm and safe, and you are riding on even ground that you can see clearly.

Riding balanced transitions between gaits is as important as changing diagonals in trot and changing leads in canter. Make sure your horse isn't pushed too hard early in the ride. Conserving his energy is necessary, especially on longer rides. It's also important for him to move with a steady rhythm to help him relax. So the rider must make sure the pace and the length of the horse's strides don't keep changing. The ideal length for the ride depends on the fitness and training level of horse and rider, as well as the ground conditions. A ride of one to two hours without stopping for a break—with appropriate intervals in walk—is reasonable for any horse in training.

SLOWING DOWN WITH CONTROL

It goes without saying that being able to slow down with control is important. When in a group, the lead rider must indicate that she plans to slow down by raising her hand so the other riders can respond in time, instead of getting too close to one another.

Canter can be a very enjoyable pace on the trail.

Taking a break: A relaxed walk on a loose rein.

The lead rider should loudly give the command, "And walk," and raise her left hand at the same time.

When the group is riding in single file, one behind the next, it's important for the safe lead horse to perform the downward transition or change of pace first. Then all the other riders should change pace, while staying two horse lengths apart from one another, as we've already discussed. Keep your hands quiet and low, and at the same time, give several half-halts until your horse slows down to the pace you are requesting. You can use a calming tone of voice as an additional aid. A deep exhalation by the rider often helps the horse to better understand the aids to slow. The rider at the back should make sure the group stays together and let the lead rider know if anybody within the group has lost control.

RIDING AWAY FROM THE GROUP

When out on the trail, various situations can arise where a rider might need to leave the group. So it's important to practice riding your horse away from the "herd."

It's best to begin by walking away from the other horses, starting with a short distance and gradually increasing it. You can do this by riding a *demi-volte*. A demi-volte is a turn that doesn't form a complete circle, so the rider ends up changing direction. Like all turns, demi-voltes are initiated and ridden using the diagonal aids. The rider uses her inside rein to bend the horse in the direction of movement; the inside leg is on the girth to push the horse into the outside rein, which gives slightly to allow him to bend. The outside leg is behind the girth to support the turn. The

RIDING AWAY FROM THE GROUP
You can start practicing riding away from the group by getting pairs of riders to set off in a different direction from the rest of the group at a crossroads or fork in the trail.

Philippa practices riding her pony away from the group.

rider puts more weight onto her inside seat bone during the turn and then sits centered again when riding out of the turn.

Because horses are herd animals, they usually don't like leaving other horses or setting off in a different direction than the group, so it's often best and safest to practice riding away from the group with another rider alongside, at first. If your horse turns and leaves the other horses willingly, give him plenty of praise so he knows he has done well.

VOLTES OR LARGE CIRCLES

Unlike a demi-volte, a *volte* is a complete, closed circle. The rider's aids are the same as for the demi-volte. Circles can be ridden in all three basic paces, but a canter circle needs to be larger than circles at slower gaits. It's always better to ride large, well-planned circles than to turn the horse without the correct bend. Horses can slip on wet ground if you make a circle too small. Tip: If a horse is getting strong and you can't keep him a safe distance from the horse in front of him, start off on a large circle, and then gradually decrease the size until he settles down.

TURN ON THE FOREHAND

Being able to turn from a halt comes in handy if you come across an obstacle you can't get past and don't want to jump over.

The aids are the same as described for the demi-volte: Turn the horse in place or on a very small circle, initiating the sideways movement of his hindquarters around his forehand with your inside leg. When in a group, once all the horses have completed a turn like this, the last rider in the group becomes the new leader.

CHANGING THE LEAD RIDER

A turn on the forehand isn't the only way to change lead rider. You can ask any rider from the group to take the lead. The rest of the group should ride in walk, while the rider who is taking the lead trots past them to reach the front.

This rider's forward aids will have to be more effective than usual to encourage the horse to change position. She should only come back to walk when she and her horse are two to four horse lengths in front of the previous lead rider.

RIDING ON THE ROAD

When traffic is a factor, you should ride at a walk with your reins short. Check the regulations for horses on the road that apply in the state and county where you are riding. When out with a large group of horses and riders, ride in single file, close behind one another and nose to tail—without the normal safety distance you would maintain on a trail—on the right-hand side of the road. In the United States, horses being ridden are typically considered vehicles, much like bicycles, and should travel in the same direction a car would travel, while unmounted horses being led are sometimes legally considered pedestrians, in which case you walk against traffic.

"To prepare for a relaxed ride on the trail, I practice with exercises in the arena at home."

Some states legally require cars and other motorized vehicles to slow or even stop in order to avoid frightening horses, but even in states where this is the case, not all drivers will necessarily be aware of the law or prepared to encounter horses along the side of the road. Typically, riders are also responsible for exercising care around moving vehicles.

CROSSING ROADS

It is best to avoid riding along the side of the road as much as possible, since passing cars can be dangerous. However, crossing roads is part of trail riding—even if you are careful to avoid riding along roads, you may still need to cross them sometimes.

You have to practice crossing roads to be able to do it safely. There are two options: If there is a quiet horse leading the group, the rider of this horse should start across, giving a hand signal to let drivers know other riders will be following her. Each rider should look left and right to see whether there are any more cars coming, and then ride across the road at a brisk walk, keeping contact with her horse's mouth. If there are any issues, it's best to deal with them by moving forward.

When riding in a group, there is another, quicker way to cross a road: If you all have a clear view of the road and can see that no traffic is coming, every rider should turn left simultaneously in response to an agreed-upon signal by the lead rider, and the entire group should ride to the other side of the road, side by side, and then fall back into line on the other side. This requires all riders to be able to turn their horses safely side by side.

You must make sure no gaps form between riders that a car could drive through. Some drivers don't know they shouldn't do this, and it could cause some horses to become separated from the group, which could lead to a dangerous situation.

Last but not least, when riding along roads and near traffic, it's always important to thank drivers for their patience. When you are across the road or have safely passed a car with your horse calm and under control, and when it is safe to do so, make eye contact and wave.

Caution: Horses are more likely to slip on concrete or paved surfaces.

Canter in a forward seat on the trail, keeping a light contact with the horse's mouth.

SAFETY FIRST

Don't put yourself in dangerous situations and don't take risks while riding out. For example, avoid unfamiliar stretches of water and never attempt to cross marshy or swampy ground. If you come across a narrow bridge, consider whether it might be better to dismount and lead your horse across. Leading is a sensible choice if your horse feels more confident with you on the ground. However, if you feel more confident in the saddle, it's better to ride. The same rule applies when a trail takes you under a low bridge, through a tunnel, or across a surface you are unsure of.

If your horse spooks at something on the trail, ride past the scary object in leg-yield or shoulder-in. If you are riding in a group, it's best to let one horse go ahead. If a horse spooks in traffic, "shield" him with a confident rider on a quiet horse: The confident rider rides close to the frightened animal on the side closest to the traffic, blocking the horse's view of the road. (This obviously only works with horses who get along and don't kick.)

Remember: When you have a horse that gets strong and can't be controlled with half-halts, you can try to settle him by riding a large circle, and then repeating it a number of times, making the circle gradually smaller.

READY FOR THE TRAIL — OUT-OF-THE-ARENA BASICS

> **PHONE RULES**
>
> It is good to have a cell phone to contact people in an emergency or to find your way if you get lost. However, making calls, writing texts, or reading when riding is not only dangerous but also rude to your horse and other riders. The same goes for wearing ear buds.

However, you need a clear, open space in order to do this. When you know your horse tends to become excited or spooky on the trail, it is a good idea to ride him in the arena first, or longe him, to get rid of some energy and calm his nerves. Then you can take him out for a ride, preferably with a quiet horse, at a walk.

Four happy, smiling faces.

Behind a relaxed lead horse, any nerves or exuberance will gradually settle, and later the group can even enjoy a steady trot and canter. Don't lose your patience, and avoid cantering too fast or for too long. Frequent long breaks in walk at an aimless meandering pace are the best way to settle nerves. Horses who become strong and excited just aren't suited to larger groups. It's a misconception that over-exuberant horses should be allowed to "get it out of their system" on the trail. It's better for them to satisfy their desire for movement out in the field, without the rider's weight. Under saddle, we want controlled movement. Make sure your horse has enough opportunity to move freely in the field. Only a calm, rideable horse can be fun and safe on the trail.

10 RULES FOR AN ENJOYABLE RIDE

1. **Safety:**
   Safe equipment for horse and rider; the rider should have adequate knowledge and skill.

2. **The horse's welfare:**
   The horse should be kept, fed, and exercised in a species-appropriate manner; he should be systematically trained and introduced to riding on the trail; he should be trained to training standard.

3. **Have a plan, and always ride out in company:**
   Plan the route for your ride in agreement with the other riders; avoid taking risks out riding; be prepared to take detours if necessary.

4. **Warm up:**
   Ride in walk for at least the first 10 to 15 minutes.

5. **Know the rules:**
   Stay on the trails; don't ride across fields; respect the laws and regulations that apply in your area.

6. **Safety in traffic:**
   Get horses used to traffic; ride in single file on the road, on the side of the road as prescribed in the traffic regulations in your state and county; only use sidewalks and cycle lanes in an emergency; wear lights when riding in the dark or in poor visibility. (This information will usually be applicable in general, but you should check the regulations for riding on the road that appy where you are riding.)

7. **Be considerate:**
   Pass pedestrians, cyclists, and other riders at walk; keep a safe distance; say "hello"; approach fields of livestock at a walk.

8. **Speed:** Ride according to the speed of the least experienced rider, and keep an eye on the ground conditions.

9. **Respect farming, hunting, and forestry:**
   Pass farm or forestry machinery at walk, avoid putting yourself at risk, and consider other people.

10. **Conservation and environmental protection:**
    Avoid riding on soft trails, fields in use, or away from marked trails without permission; divert around cultivated biotopes; don't disturb wild bird or animal nests.

ALWAYS RIDE AS A TEAM

A relaxed ride in a loose group formation.

Walking on a loose rein.

Slight flexion with a light contact can work well on the trail.

Photo Feature — Always Ride as a Team

When the horses in a group get along, you can ride alongside each other.

At the end of the ride, all the horses should be walking contentedly, with relaxed riders.

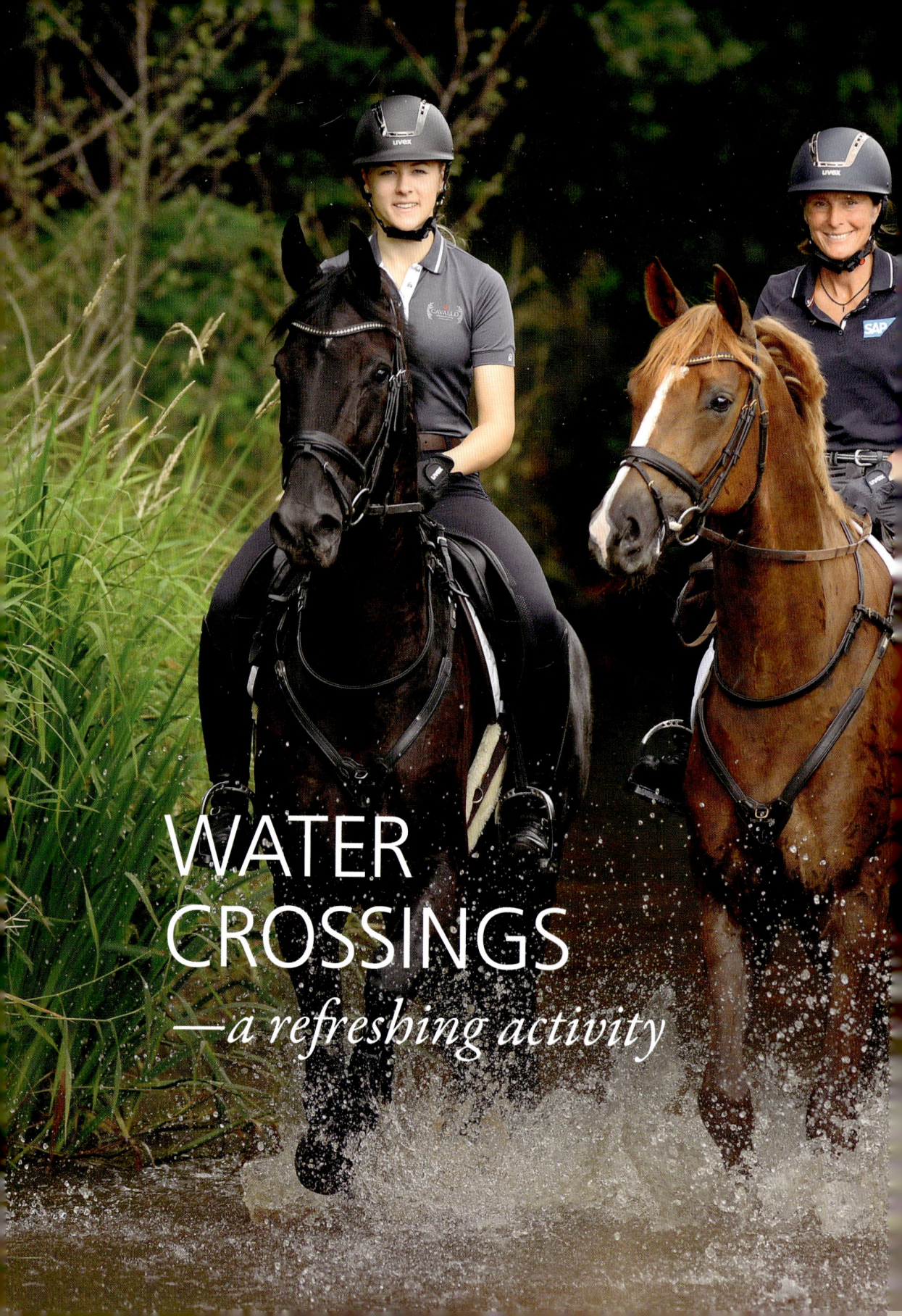

WATER CROSSINGS
—a refreshing activity

After it rains, find some big puddles to canter through!

GETTING USED TO WATER

AN ESSENTIAL EXERCISE

I take the time to gradually get my horses used to water. Crossing water is an important skill for all horses and something that my horses must do. Dressage horses need to perform movements obediently, without being distracted or worried by puddles in the arena. A heavy shower can leave a show jumping course underwater, so show jumpers can't let water bother them, either. And eventers obviously need to be able to jump boldly into water and even canter through it (more about this later!). That's why I try to incorporate riding through different types of water into as many rides as possible. In the summer months, riding through water is a refreshing activity that benefits horses and riders and is always welcome.

START WITH A LEAD HORSE

The first thing you need to do is make sure the water you are crossing isn't too deep and the ground conditions are good. Young horses will find it easier to take their first wet steps in a group, behind an experienced lead horse. (Be sure to maintain a safe distance from other horses in water.) You will find that most horses enjoy going into water once they get over any initial worries. Some horses like to drink, while others like to splash or even try to roll.

When getting a horse used to water for the first time, you need a good lead horse who will go into the water and won't kick if another horse comes too close to him. An inexperienced horse might suddenly decide to leap into the water. If that happens, he could end up getting too close to the lead horse.

Crossing water is easy if an experienced lead horse goes first. Younger horses or riders should follow closely behind. The horses should progressively work up to walking confidently alongside each other.

WATER CROSSINGS — GETTING USED TO WATER

Start by approaching the water at a walk, approximately two horse lengths behind the lead horse. Ideally, your horse should follow the lead horse into the water. If he hesitates, wait a moment and allow him to have a sniff on a long rein. Then ask him to go forward again and follow the lead horse.

Encourage your horse with your voice and leg. As soon as he takes a step in the direction of the water, praise him, and give him a pat to encourage him. An inexperienced horse will probably be able to pull himself together on his second attempt and start to follow the lead horse, albeit hesitantly. Stand in the middle of the water and give your horse lots of praise. He will have a sniff, and might even dip his muzzle into the water or have a drink. Let your reins slip through your fingers and wait. If your horse tries to paw or splash, ride forward. Holes in the ground caused by pawing are dangerous, and pawing is often a precursor to getting down to roll.

Have the lead horse leave the water and ride on in walk, and then follow him, one behind the other. If your horse follows willingly and walks behind the lead horse without stopping, have the lead horse return to the water. Ride the inexperienced horse out of the water and then ride back into it—this time on your own while the experienced horse remains standing in the water.

WALK, THEN TROT, THEN CANTER

The next step is to trot into the water behind the experienced horse. Some horses don't like the spray from the horse in front of them, so you need to be prepared for hesitation or stopping. Then trot through the water without the lead horse. You should post in the trot to take strain off the horse's back.

Some horses enjoy water crossings right from the outset. You should always make use of this motivation, especially in warm weather, because riding through water has a handy cooling effect on the horse's legs.

Even by himself, Mustang canters boldly through the water with his ears pricked.

GRETA AND SCRABBLE IN THE WATER

Standing in water not only cools off a horse's legs but also creates trust. You should test the ground at a walk before trying the crossing at a canter.

Greta rides into the water in a controlled canter.

Scrabble is an experienced horse who isn't bothered by spray.

Photo Feature — Greta and Scrabble in the Water

Pure enjoyment!

ENJOYING WATER IN DIFFERENT WAYS

Firlefranz and Bobby are relaxed and content as they walk through the water together.

Photo Feature — Enjoying Water in Different Ways

Bobby enjoys drinking from the stream.

Firle likes splashing.

Unexpected visitors: We were surprised on this ride by a couple of wild horses.

JUMPING OBSTACLES
—outside the arena

PREPARING FOR JUMPING

In the previous chapters, we discussed basic rules for staying safe when riding on the trail. Next, I'm going to show you how to tackle jumping outside the arena. Before I or my students jump obstacles on the trail, we warm up the horses in an enclosed field.

ALWAYS BEGIN IN WALK

As in every warm-up phase, spend 10 to 15 minutes riding in walk on a loose rein. You can ride alongside each other in pairs or spread out, and let the horses have a look at

A back protector and breastplate with an integrated neck strap help keep you safe when you are jumping outside the arena.

Take the time to show your horse the different jumps. Let him look at the jumps and sniff them. This will help you jump them safely later on.

the jumps or sniff them to help them get used to these potentially new objects.

If your horse becomes strong and excited, ride in walk with the longest rein possible. This will give you and your horse confidence. It's important to keep both hands firmly on the reins, even during free walk on a loose rein. The trail can be full of surprises. An animal could pop out of the bushes at any moment.

Ride with your stirrups two holes shorter when jumping oustide the arena. Also make sure the bottom strap of your horse's breastplate (if he wears one) fits tightly between his front legs. Under no circumstances should it form a loop that the horse could get his leg caught in; this could cause him to fall on landing after a jump. I only use a martingale in exceptional circumstances when riding on the trail—for example, when a pony is too strong for a child.

The breastplate should not dangle between the horse's front legs but fit snugly, as shown here.

JUMPING OBSTACLES — PREPARING FOR JUMPING

WARM UP IN RISING TROT

After riding in walk, warm the horses up in rising trot. Always remember that the aim is for the horse to relax and stretch down into the contact. Ride big lines and changes of rein. You can also incorporate riding in between the jumps. Remember to ride the turns in a nice, active working trot. When turning to the left, the left leg pushes the horse into the bend and the outside rein controls the bend, with the hand quiet and low, and the heel kept still. Your calves should lie flat against the horse's sides. Keep a secure contact on both reins, so you always have an even and consistent connection to the horse's mouth. Maintain an even rhythm in the trot. Keep your hands low, and invite the horse to take the reins all the way to the buckle. Then come back to walk.

PREPARATORY CANTER WORK

Begin cantering in a forward seat, with your hands low at the withers. Feel free to ride a few transitions within the pace. Canter forward in a light seat on straight lines and then sit back down in the saddle to slow down. This teaches the horse to slow down and collect the canter when you sit in the saddle. Then ride a change of rein, so you've practiced the transitions on both reins. During this exercise, aim to bring the horse's hindquarters under his center of gravity.

The two calm lead horses trot in front.

Warming up in canter in a forward seat, in a group alongside each other.

SEAT POSITION AND SPEED

Always stay in a forward seat between jumps, to take strain off the horse's back. All the rider's weight should be in her heels. If you aren't sure how far forward you should be, it helps to imagine standing on the floor with your knees bent. If you incline your upper body too far forward, you'll fall over. If you're too upright, you'll tip backward. So imagine you're standing with your knees bent, positioned so that you're always able to keep your balance. This is the perfect angle for your upper body in the forward seat.

When you come to a jump, sit in the saddle like a dressage rider—grow tall in your upper body, and signal to the horse that he should collect the canter, bring his hindquarters underneath his center of gravity, and reduce the speed. Return to a forward seat and canter away after the jump. Changes in pace in different seat positions quickly teach the horse that he can canter forward more freely after the jump with his rider in a forward seat, and that he needs to collect himself before the jump when the rider reduces speed.

CONTROL AND STOPPING

Before you begin jumping, make sure you can control your horse. Maintain an even contact with the horse's mouth on both reins. However, your horse's nose shouldn't be behind the vertical, and he should be able to look at the jump. The canter should be active, but you should still be able to stop at any time. Practice coming back to trot, to walk, and then to halt, so you learn to stay in control. Then give with the reins, but only ride forward again when you want to and not when your horse wants to, so he learns to listen to your commands.

Canter in a rhythm in a forward seat; then start using your weight aid and sit down, coming back to trot, walk, and then halt, and praise your horse. Once you have control, you can start jumping.

> **BE CAREFUL WITH YOUR WHIP**
>
> Not holding your whip properly can be dangerous. If you hold your whip too far down, with the end poking out of your hand, it could get tangled up in your reins. Or, even worse, if your horse stops and you tip forward, you could injure yourself on the end of the whip. So always hold the whip at the top.

The horse should always have at least one ear on the rider.

SUMMARY

Start by giving your horse a good warm-up in a fenced-in field. Walk on a loose rein for 10 to 15 minutes, then transition into a rising trot, staying long and low around the jumps. Then work on transitions in canter. Practice collecting and lengthening the canter stride before you start jumping. Riding on bending lines—circling—is also effective. Your horse should be relaxed and listening to your aids before you start jumping. It's also important to practice stopping. The rider should always be in control and should always be able to bring the horse from canter back to trot, then walk, and finally halt. This is important for safety reasons.

Hands perpendicular to the eyes, in a forward seat, with the weight in the heels. The rider looks between the horse's ears to the next jump.

POSITION AND PLAN

BASIC RULES

Now we can begin jumping outside the arena. However, there are still a few things to keep in mind. As the rider, you are responsible for choosing the correct approach. That means you need to look at the obstacle from a distance away, and ride straight toward the middle. The approach and speed are up to you. Ride in a forward seat, staying in a rhythmical, working-to-medium canter between obstacles. Don't ride too fast when you are training; maintain an even and controlled rhythm. Slow down if your horse gets too fast, and ride more forward if he is too slow. It's up to the horse to decide what happens at the jump itself. He must take responsibility, too; after all, horse and rider are supposed to be a partnership. It's about 50-50 between the rider looking out for the horse and the horse looking out for the rider.

The safety seat: Toes in front of the knees; weight in the stirrups, with the heels down. The reins could be a little longer here, in order to bring the hands below the eyes.

When cantering in a forward seat between obstacles, always make sure your hands are perpendicular to your eyes. They should be above the withers, not too far forward. Know how to use the "safety seat" when you jump. That means your toes come farther forward than your knees as you land. It's easier if you sit farther back in the saddle, with your reins long enough that the horse can use his neck to balance, both in the canter and when jumping. Always have your weight in the stirrups. It's crucial to keep your weight in your heels so your feet can absorb your weight on landing. You should land with your weight on your stirrups, not on your horse's back.

It's also important to "bridge your reins." Hold both reins in your right hand, so that you have the right rein in your hand with the left rein directly on top of it, or vice versa. Keep your thumbs on top. The space between your right hand and your left hand should be the width of a fist. You can then support yourself on the horse's neck in an emergency, which will prevent you from tipping forward, without dropping your reins

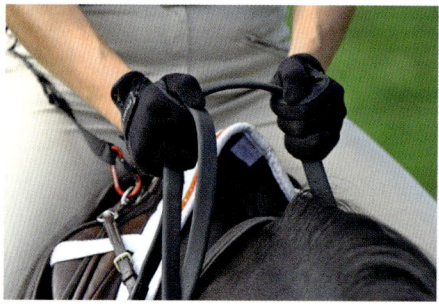

Bridging your reins when jumping outside the arena is done with one hand. This makes it easier to lengthen and shorten your reins.

completely. And when you turn the horse, you will automatically use the outside rein to turn, instead of just the inside, so you control the horse's outside shoulder. If you lose your balance, grab the neck strap immediately and allow your reins to slip slightly. Under no circumstances should you use the reins to balance yourself.

As mentioned, it is important to have your reins long enough for the horse to use his body in the jump and so if your horse stumbles or bucks after a jump, you aren't pulled out of your seat. Loosen your fingers and let the reins slip through them so the horse doesn't pull you forward. Safety comes first when riding over jumps outside the arena.

SUMMARY

Canter in a forward seat between obstacles. Always keep looking forward toward the next obstacle. Keep your reins long enough, while always maintaining a consistent contact with the horse's mouth. You should feel springy pressure in your heels. Your seat should be closer to the saddle as you approach an obstacle. Gather up your horse and bring him more over his center of gravity. Stay in balance with your horse over the jump. Keep your hands perpendicular to your eyes. Make sure your stirrups absorb your weight when you land. Your toes should be in front of your knees. Ride on in a forward seat after landing, and bridge your reins.

Remember, when jumping out on a ride, the rider is generally responsible for choosing the right approach and the right pace.

GUIDELINES TO REMEMBER

Rider Responsibilities

— Choose the correct **pace** for the type of obstacle.

— Focus on the ideal **line** and the best approach.

— Use the weight, leg, and rein aids to bring the horse into **balance**.

— Keep the **reins** long enough to allow your horse to use his neck to **balance** without pulling you forward.

— Ensure your horse is **always in front of the forward aids**. Surprise transitions are also helpful.

— Ensure your horse canters actively **under his center of gravity**, especially on **turns and during changes of pace**.

The Different Seats

— **Forward seat:** Between jumps.

— **Seat on the approach:** Upright seat, closer to the saddle.

— **Seat on landing:** Also called the "landing seat" or "safety seat," with your weight in your stirrups, your toes in front of your knees, and your center of gravity behind the stirrups; look forward between your horse's ears, and make sure the reins are long enough.

— **The "Oh, crap!" seat:** Used to recover if the horse trips or stumbles.

THE CHRIS BARTLE "OH, CRAP!" SEAT

British equestrian Chris Bartle's now-famous advice for hairy situations is the "oh, crap!" seat, which is like the safety seat. The rider should sit as far back in the saddle as possible. The toes should be on an imaginary line in front of the knees, with the lower legs far forward. The rider's seat is in the saddle, with the upper body behind the vertical. The hands should be perpendicular to the rider's eyes. Chris Bartle says that, to achieve this, you can "push your hands against the withers." The reins should be long enough to allow the horse to use his neck to balance. The rider can only lean far enough back with her upper body and give the horse enough freedom in his shoulder if the reins are long.

RIDER REQUIREMENTS

The rider will need good upper and lower leg strength, as well as good muscle tone in general, to manage all the seat positions mentioned in this chapter. You need to learn how to activate your core muscles. The rider also needs to practice quickly slipping and gathering up the reins so you can do it instantly and, above all, instinctively, without dropping them.

Bridged reins add a safety element over cross-country jumps.

We trot one behind another along an undulating track.

CROSS-COUNTRY OBSTACLES

UNDULATING TRACK

The first element to consider is the likelihood of an undulating track when jumping outside the arena. Riding over consecutive hills improves both the horse's and the rider's sense of balance. They also both learn to maintain an even rhythm going uphill and downhill. It's excellent preparation for trail riding, but also for taking off and landing after jumps.

Find a rolling field or track with gentle slopes to negotiate. Start by bridging your reins. Then practice both sitting and posting the trot as you traverse your undulating track.

Maintain an even pace in trot. The horse isn't allowed to go faster downhill or slower uphill. You might need to steady up or push on to maintain an even pace.

Next you can try cantering. Incline your upper body forward slightly when going uphill. Sit up tall when riding downhill, with your lower leg forward and your hands low. Make sure you can balance well in a forward seat when cantering along the track. Your horse shouldn't lose energy when going uphill or go faster when going downhill.

This exercise helps improve your balance and your feel for an even canter rhythm.

The first logs you jump should be very low.

LOGS

Small logs are a good place to begin when jumping outside the arena. Even if you just go out for an easy trail ride, you might find a fallen tree blocking your way. That's why it's useful to prepare yourself and your horse to safely tackle small cross-country obstacles. These first "natural obstacles" should be very small; your horse should be able to step over them in an emergency. These obstacles should preferably be very long, too, and are even better with small trees or jump standards at each end. In other words, you should make jumping the obstacle as easy as possible for your horse.

If your horse hesitates or stops at first, you need to make it clear to him that he must get to the other side of the obstacle, even from a standstill. That's why you should start with very small jumps.

The same principle always applies to jumping different obstacles on the trail: Start by approaching in walk and let the horse sniff the strange obstacle. Then take up the reins and bridge them. The bridge shouldn't be too wide. An inexperienced rider or horse should always start off by following an experienced lead horse. Trot two horse lengths behind the lead horse, in rising trot. Look at the jump and go into sitting trot in a light seat—early enough so you don't get ahead of the movement and jump before the horse. Always allow the horse to jump first and go with his movement.

JUMPING OBSTACLES — CROSS-COUNTRY OBSTACLES

This inexperienced horse over-jumps.

Some horses tend to buck or run away after a jump out of pure high spirits, especially when they are young and green. Adopt the safety seat and use your bridged reins to prevent the horse from getting his head down and bucking. Riding forward can sometimes also be effective. If your horse becomes too strong after a jump, try to regain control by riding a circle. It's also advisable to come back to a slower pace after the jump so the horse can't evade your aids.

Approach the obstacle in a straight line from a good distance, allowing the horse to look at the jump. Maintain a light contact with the horse's mouth so you can intervene if he tries to duck out to the side.

Once you have jumped behind a lead horse without hesitating three or four times, you can try to jump the obstacle from a trot by yourself. It's easier to begin with if the group or the lead horse stands behind the jump.

If your horse stays under control in trot, without rushing toward the jump or running away after it, you can try approaching again from a steady canter.

If he does get too strong, try approaching the obstacle on a turn so your horse is only straight in front of it for three to four horse lengths. Make sure you maintain an even rhythm on the turn.

A joyful buck often comes with the territory.

55

JUMPING OBSTACLES — CROSS-COUNTRY OBSTACLES

Once you've jumped the log from canter a few times, take a breather in walk. It's important to praise your horse after every good jump. This helps build confidence and gives him encouragement.

BRUSH FENCES

Brush fences are a classic example of the type of natural obstacle people enjoy jumping when out hunting. The fence is stuffed with brushes so the horse can push through the higher part. This is something horses learn through experience. They often start off over-jumping, because they don't have the confidence to push through the brush instead. To prevent excessive over-jumping, you should avoid beginning with brush fences that are too high. Over-jumping takes a lot of energy, and results in an exaggerated sequence of movement; the rider will need a secure seat to compensate for it.

Cautious horses sometimes need longer before they can jump economically. Brush over the solid element of an obstacle is often used for safety purposes on cross-country courses because it makes horses jump a little higher. In hairy situations, the horse can jump through the brush, reducing the risk of injury.

Philippa's pony jumps safely over the middle of this wide, low brush fence.

It's a bit scary! This horse takes a big leap and looks down at the ditch.

No problem! Experienced Nemo confidently jumps the ditch.

DITCHES

Ditches are obstacles you can come across on any trail ride. They can look intimidating, especially if they're deep or full of water. If you have an inexperienced horse, then you can't afford to make any mistakes in the first few training sessions. Inexperienced horses need experienced riders. If the rider is unsure, the horse will immediately pick up on it. It's normal for a horse to hesitate at his first ditch. You need to support him by riding forward decisively and follow a lead horse until he can jump confidently.

Inexperienced or nervous riders need confident, experienced horses and should only start jumping ditches once they can confidently manage other obstacles.

The ideal ditch for first attempts should be dry and a maximum of 2½ to 3 feet (0.8 to 1 m) wide so the horse can still jump it from a standstill if need be. Check first to make sure the edge of the ditch is clearly visible, and not overgrown with grass or weeds. The horse must be able to clearly make out the takeoff spot, as well as the rear boundary. On cross-country courses, you will often see a white painted border that discourages the horse from stepping on the edge of the ditch.

Up to this point, we've let inexperienced horses walk up to strange obstacles to have a look at them. Ditches are an exception to this rule. We don't let horses look and sniff first because it's how ditches look that makes them a bit scary. But jumping a ditch is basically just an extended canter stride.

Mustang and Philippa take a long jump over a ditch and log.

Start off in trot behind a lead horse. Horses will often jump a ditch confidently the first time. But as they go over it, they notice it underneath them, and the next time around, they take a giant leap, hesitate, or stop. So you need to pay attention, not the first time, but rather the second. Support your horse positively with your leg and keep your reins long enough, but not too long, so your horse keeps his head up and doesn't look down into the ditch. You should always have the horse in front of your leg. It's also important to have a bit of extra impulsion because that will help your horse jump over the ditch.

What if your horse stops at the ditch? Approach the ditch again, decisively, at a flowing pace behind a lead horse if possible. Keep your reins short so your horse concentrates on your aids. Be prepared for hesitation, and ride in sitting trot so you can use the leg aids more effectively. Your forward aids must make up for the horse's indecisiveness if he hesitates. You can back up your leg aids with your voice—for example, by clicking your tongue or saying, "Come on!" It's important to be consistent in your approach; this is the only way to prevent a refusal.

It's okay to follow the lead horse over a ditch more times than for other obstacles. An inexperienced horse might not refuse until the last moment, when he spots the ditch. If the lead horse is already on the other side of the ditch, your horse might suddenly decide to take off after all. You need to be ready for anything, and grab the neck strap if necessary.

If your horse jumps the ditch, come back to trot and then walk, and praise him with your voice and a neck scratch. Take a quick breather in walk, and then keep practicing until your horse confidently jumps the ditch with no hesitation. Make sure you don't ask too much of your horse physically.

SUMMARY

Always follow this basic principle when jumping out on the trail: Show your horse the obstacle first. Allow a more experienced horse to take the lead over the obstacle, and follow him. Then try it by yourselves. Start with the lead horse waiting on the other side, and then jump the obstacle without the lead horse. Low, inviting, fallen tree trunks are a good place to start. Choose one that's low enough for your horse to step over in walk. It should be long and have bushes or wings at either side. Lower obstacles with brush also good for beginners.

Once you are confidently jumping fallen trees and brush fences with no hesitation, you can try your first ditch. It's best to start jumping ditches in combination with a log. Approach the obstacle so the ditch is behind the log, and then repeat it a few times. Then you can try approaching it from the other direction. Careful! Ditches invite horses to look into them. Be ready for your horse to perform a slightly bigger jump than he needs. Keep looking forward between the horse's ears, not down into the ditch.

Pricked ears and an eager expression show the horse's enjoyment.

JUMPING OBSTACLES — CROSS-COUNTRY OBSTACLES

STEPS AND BANKS

Steps and banks are classic cross-country obstacles. You might also find yourself having to jump up or down a step or small bank while out on the trail. I'm going to show you two examples of this type of obstacle, and explain the right way to approach and safely tackle them.

Whether you start by jumping up or down a step depends on your individual training setup. If your training area has a sunken portion, you will have to jump down first before jumping back up. The other variation is a bank, where you jump up first and then jump back down. The most important thing is to start at the lowest level.

Confidently jumping up the step...

JUMPING UP

What do you need to think about when jumping up a step or bank? It's important for the rider not to end up behind the movement. An inexperienced rider should hold the neck strap if she feels unsure. It's always better to hold the neck strap than to risk interfering with the horse's mouth! Incline your upper body forward when riding up a step, as you did when riding the undulating track described earlier in this chapter. Make sure the pace doesn't increase when jumping up; maintain rhythm, and allow your upper body to go forward as if you were going over a jump. You need to approach a step up at an energetic pace, which shouldn't be confused with a fast, flat canter.

Some horses find jumping up and down easy. They usually tend to have naturally good coordination and balance. A horse with a weak back or poor balance will need to practice this kind of obstacle in smaller steps.

The second variation on this theme is a bank or raised platform. An inexperienced horse should follow a lead horse in trot, and the rider should let him have a look at the step. The pace must be energetic enough; horses need to push off hard to jump up, so their hindquarters must be activated. However, it's important not to lose impulsion, so you shouldn't over-collect the horse either. Some horses find it difficult to judge when to take off, at first.

If your horse refuses, let him sniff the step. Never try to make him jump up from a standstill. If your horse stops in front of a step up, approach it again from a distance with plenty of impulsion. If your horse hesitates even slightly, it's essential to ride forward so you don't lose any impulsion. If your horse jumps up, bring him back to walk and praise him. Ride the next attempt without following the lead horse, but with the lead horse standing either on or behind the bank. The lead horse shouldn't stand next to the takeoff or on the approach, in order to prevent your horse from becoming "sticky" (tentative). When you're practicing jumping up, approaching from canter can be a good idea, because many horses find jumping up easier from canter.

and coming back to walk on top of the bank.

JUMPING DOWN

How to jump a step down: Start by approaching in walk or even jumping down from halt. You need to approach at a steady pace, because your horse is supposed to jump down slowly and carefully. Your reins should be long enough to allow him to use his neck to balance.

The rider can maintain contact with the horse's mouth, even with longer reins. Your reins must never be too short. To stay in balance with the horse, the rider should sit tall and almost lean back slightly with her upper body. The rider's weight shouldn't be on the forehand. The rider should be sitting the trot, so as not to get in front of the horse's movement.

When the horse jumps down, open your fingers and let the reins slip through slightly. Remember to keep your toes forward and to land with your weight in your heels. Make sure you don't land heavily on the horse's back. That's often easier said than done, when first trying these obstacles.

SUMMARY

Let's go back over what we've covered here: If possible, always practice jumping up first. Keep an even rhythm and don't allow your horse to speed up. Stay in balance with your horse's movement. When you try the first steps down, remember to keep your upper body upright and to slip your reins at the right time. This is important because it allows the horse to use his neck to balance. Let the stirrups absorb your weight on landing. Keep looking forward and not down.

Keep your upper body vertical when landing after a step or bank...

... and only lean forward again once you've landed.

SMALL CROSS-COUNTRY OBSTACLES

The young pony's hesitation shows how important the lead pony is.

A relaxed canter over a small log ...

... and a brave jump over a bigger one.

Photo Feature — Small Cross-Country Obstacles

The first small obstacles you try should be very wide.

A coop...

... and a gate.

BRUSH FENCES

Low, wide brush fences ...   *... are ideal for beginners.*

This brush fence over a ditch is for more experienced riders.

COMPETITION OBSTACLES

Cascamara demonstrating good foreleg technique.

Siena with her ears pricked: Only flying could be more fun.

Professor Bobby showing how it's done over an oxer with an MIM frangible pin system.

JUMPING INTO AND OUT OF WATER

We've already tackled getting horses used to water, and your horse is now able to go into and through water as a matter of course. If your horse is still hesitant about going into water, find a bold lead horse for him to follow. Your reins can be a little longer, to allow your horse to have a look at and sniff the water. If he doesn't want to go in, it can be helpful for the rest of the group to ride past you into the water. Your horse will want to keep up with the group.

If you go through water on every trail ride, your horse will soon lose his fear of getting his feet wet. Once your horse can walk, trot, and canter into and through water without any issues, you can add in the excitement of jumping in and out. You should always start by riding into water and then jumping out. Your horse will then find it easier to jump into water.

Horses who are still hesitant and won't canter through water independently will need a lead horse to jump into the water first. Make sure you keep enough distance between the two horses. You never know how horses will react to their first jump into water. Some horses will take a massive leap right into it. Because experienced horses tend to jump more economically, this situation can be dangerous for the lead horse if you don't keep your horse two to three horse lengths away from him. If your horse is a bold type and you have spent time getting him used to water, you can make your first attempt without a lead horse.

Walking into water is easier in company.

Horses feel more confident in a group.

I trot and canter my horses through water before I start jumping into it.

PREPARATION

How should you prepare? After warming up and jumping some familiar obstacles, ride down a few steps or a bank at a steady pace. Riding down steps prepares the horse for jumping down into water. Practice the correct position by letting your reins slip through your fingers and keeping your upper body upright. The forward-downward pressure in your heels and the safety seat form the basis for a safe landing.

Your toes should always be in front of your knees. You should also trot and canter through splashing water a few times from both sides.

RULE OF WATER

Give young, inexperienced horses the chance to get used to water by trotting and cantering through it before asking them to jump into it.

JUMPING OBSTACLES — JUMPING INTO AND OUT OF WATER

WHAT TO DO

1. Start by jumping out of water to get your horse used to the feel and the ground conditions underwater. If possible, a low log makes a good first jump out of water.

2. Once your horse is cantering fluidly through the water and jumping confidently out over a log, you can try jumping over a log into water.

3. The first drop into water shouldn't be too big. A low step that can be ridden from trot to begin with is enough.

This step-by-step approach is important to prevent you from asking too much of yourself or your horse. You don't have to achieve all these steps in one training session. You will be on the safe side if your horse manages each new step two to three times and jumps confidently. Some horses will take longer to get used to each new exercise. You should only go to the second step with them, and leave the rest for a later date.

You should only jump into water from a steady pace, because the water will have a considerable braking effect on the horse's impulsion. It's safest to approach in trot at first. You will need to sit up tall to stay in balance with the horse. Your reins must be long enough to allow the horse complete freedom to balance with his neck (as for jumping drops).

WHAT CAN HAPPEN?

The horse might lose his nerve and stop. If that happens, you need to follow a lead horse again and ride forward energetically. If your horse is unsure and can't pluck up the courage to continue, it's best to go back a step and start again from the beginning. Sometimes it's worthwhile to canter through water a few times without jumping. Only try jumping out of water again when your horse can canter through it without hesitating.

If an inexperienced horse stops at the log and doesn't want to jump down over it, approach it again. You should keep approaching low obstacles until a relaxed takeoff shows you that the horse is feeling confident. When things go wrong, you must go back to the beginning and walk in and out of the water to help your horse get over his fright.

When you jump into water, it's important to slip your reins at the right time to allow your horse to stretch his neck.

WATER JUMPS

Look forward through the horse's ears ...

... or at the next jump.

Slip your reins when jumping into water so your horse can stretch his neck.

Photo Feature — Water Jumps

Your reins must also be long enough when jumping out of water.

Praise motivates your horse and gives him confidence ...

... and makes both horse and rider smile.

FITNESS TRAINING
—*outside the arena*

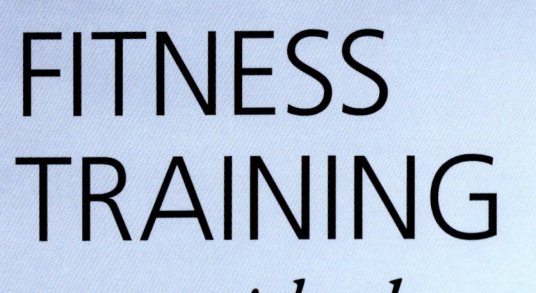

STRENGTH AND CONDITIONING

START SLOWLY

Even during the winter months, my trail group rides as often as the weather allows—at least once a week, to build up a basic level of fitness with long stretches of trot and canter. Even extensive work at walk in between rides or riding over small hills and undulating ground benefits the horse's fitness. This can be integrated into training without too much effort. Even small bumps in the ground improve balance and allow the horse to experience a different kind of movement from flat arena footing. This is why I regularly incorporate uphill and downhill slopes into my training, whether it's on an undulating track with cross-country jumps or with regular training on hills.

A calm, balanced canter uphill.

Controlled trotting in a group.

RIDING UP AND DOWN HILLS

Riding up and down hills helps to develop strength and improves the horse's balance, suppleness, and surefootedness. If you ride a young, inexperienced horse up a slope, he will initially increase his pace to gather momentum, and when he gets to the top, he will slow down because he loses momentum. Most horses tend to speed up when ridden downhill. In this case, the rider will have to slow the pace. You want your horse to maintain an even pace, both uphill and downhill.

Riding downhill in walk.

Riding up and downhill strengthens all the muscles in the horse's body, improves stamina, and is good for the horse's balance and surefootedness.

Support from the rider in the form of the correct seat is very important. When riding uphill, the rider inclines her upper body forward to take her weight off the horse's hindquarters, which need to work harder. Ride downhill in a straight line, not perpendicular to the slope. If the hill is very steep, ride at the walk; otherwise, stick to a steady trot if possible. When it comes to your seat, don't go with the horse's movement too much, don't lean forward exaggeratedly with your upper body, and don't shift too much weight onto the horse's forehand.

Make sure you don't ask too much of your horse physically. There is a much higher risk of this out on the trail, especially when you're riding with other horses. Horses encourage each other and like to keep up with each other in a group. The decrease in your horse's energy as he tires will be harder to feel out on a trail ride than in an indoor or outdoor arena. That's why it's always important to start slowly and not ask for too much too soon. Listen to your horse and pay attention to his breathing.

DON'T PUSH

Allow your horse to set the pace to begin with, and don't push him on an uphill slope. Always introduce young horses to work on hills slowly and gently so as not to overtax them.

FITNESS TRAINING — STRENGTH AND CONDITIONING

WORKING ON SLOPES

I start working on slopes with our horses as soon as the weather allows—by March, at the latest. Ideally, we go to train on hills every five days. We start off with 10 to 15 minutes of warm-up in walk. Even this is good training for all the horse's muscles. When we ride uphill, horses must push off energetically with their hind legs and use all their back muscles. Make sure you don't start off riding up and down hills that are too steep. Your horse needs the chance to slowly get used to the new demands on his body. You can gradually increase the angle of incline you work him on, with regular training. After the warm-up phase in walk, we trot at a steady pace for around 10 to 15 minutes, trotting both uphill and downhill.

Horses often find hill training at the beginning of the season exciting because there are lots of new sights, sounds, and smells to take in.

HILLY TERRAIN

Riding on hilly terrain is the best way to strengthen the horse's musculature, especially in the back and hindquarters. You can ride in walk, trot, or canter, depending on the horse's level of training.

Warm-up phase in walk on a loose rein.

FITNESS TRAINING — STRENGTH AND CONDITIONING

When riding uphill, the rider should lean forward slightly. Her weight should be in the stirrups, with her heels down. Her hands should be low, with the reins long enough that the horse can use his neck to balance. The steeper the slope, the more balanced the rider's seat must be. This makes it easier for the horse to carry the rider's weight uphill. When riding up very steep slopes, it helps to hold the neck strap and stand up in your stirrups. When riding downhill, the rider should lean back slightly to keep her weight over the horse's center of gravity. It takes a lot of effort for a horse to brake, so the rider will need to contain him with her aids.

CANTER WORK

After the trot phase, we begin cantering at a steady pace. Horses who are familiar with this exercise usually accelerate; the steeper the hill, the faster they go. Young horses, by contrast, usually run out of steam more quickly and fall back into trot.

Allow your horse to set the pace to begin with. Always introduce all horses to canter work on slopes slowly and gently so as not to overtax them. Constantly riding up and downhill requires a high level of concentration and surefootedness.

We consider the horses' training level when putting together a group to ride out together.

Interval training enables me to focus specifically on fitness and performance.

Cantering in a group risks the horses catching each other's enthusiasm and winding each other up, so, if riding with others, it's a good idea to keep the size of the group small. We only canter horses at a similar training level together. You need to consider the horse's personality, in addition to his level of training. For example, enthusiastic Bobby never wants to be overtaken by another horse. If another horse tries to overtake him, he doesn't just canter faster—he bucks. Other horses will happily canter at the back of a group. Asha and Siena, for example, are easy to control at the back.

The more often horses canter uphill, the fitter and stronger they become. This might well make them much more enthusiastic and motivated, and you will have to rethink the composition of your group as a result.

Start your canter training calmly with a stretch of no more than two minutes. If your horse still has enough energy, you can canter uphill again after taking a three-minute break in walk. Then you can canter on and trot for another five to ten minutes before coming back to walk. Ride in walk until your horse's pulse and respiratory rate have returned to normal.

INTERVAL TRAINING

I normally do interval training every five days with my event horses, to improve their fitness and performance for cross-country competition. I find five days to be ideal timing because the horse's body needs to receive training stimuli in between interval sessions to enable it to adapt to the increased workload.

FITNESS TRAINING — STRENGTH AND CONDITIONING

Starting up the hill at a steady pace.

Reaching the top of the hill, still in canter.

Five days gives the horse a long enough recovery phase; on the days in between interval sessions, I do dressage, jumping, and, of course, cavalletti training. The day after canter training is a rest day. The horses have either a day off where they are turned out in the field, or only gentle exercise or a longeing session.

We begin interval training as we do with any hill work, with 15 minutes in walk, followed by 10 to 15 minutes of rising trot. I begin the first canter phase at a steady pace, and then increase it slowly. Sprints only come at the end of the training session. Chris Bartle once told me, "Speed kills." For that reason, I only ride short, fast phases when intensifying training before a long competition.

We finish an interval training day with a steady canter, a steady trot, and plenty of walk.

INTERVAL PARAMETERS

I generally divide up my interval training into three canter intervals, with three-minute breaks in walk or trot between each. The duration and distance of the individual canter intervals depend on the training ground. Both speed and incline affect heart rate. Parameters are the number of repetitions and breaks in between, the time (two to three minutes), and the pace (trot or walk), as well as the ground conditions. Fitness consists of stamina, strength, and speed. Basic stamina work is followed by strength training, and finally speed training.

BUILDING FITNESS WITH CANTER WORK

Full of enthusiasm for canter work.

Scrabble's canter really covers the ground.

Springtime is when I lay the fitness foundations for the coming season.

Photo Feature — Building Fitness with Canter Work

Cascamara at full speed ...

... powerful and dynamic.

The first spring event competitions also help build fitness for later in the season.

SUPPLING
—outside the arena

DRESSAGE OUT ON THE TRAIL

BENEFITS

I regularly ride my dressage horses out on the trail. Not only does it benefit them mentally, it also benefits them physically in different ways. I believe varied training benefits every horse, regardless of discipline. This is something I use trail riding for.

On the following pages, I tell you about some of the ways you can use the energy and fresh air of the open country in your training to give your dressage horse motivation, strength, and expression when ridden in the arena. Riding out will also benefit his composure and nerves. And riding on different surfaces—sand, grass; dry, muddy—will improve your horse's balance and surefootedness.

There's lots for Franziskus to see out on the trail.

Franziskus enjoys a canter without fences.

The hills, undulations, hollows, and slopes can improve your horse's physical suppleness and use of his back.

You can also work on changes of pace on hills, and use gravity to help you develop extension and collection. Riding downhill has a collecting effect and gets the horse to shift his weight onto his hindquarters without you having to do much. You will notice how riding your horse up a steep slope strengthens his musculature much more effectively than riding on a level surface. Moving off perfectly manicured ground and venturing onto forest tracks or uneven hillsides with roots, branches, or puddles will not only make your horse more surefooted and agile, but also more alert and therefore more accepting of your aids.

I know that dressage riders in particular will have to steel themselves to do this out of fear that their horse will trip or injure himself if the footing is less than perfect. But, however counterintuitive it may seem, the more I ride on different surfaces—including uneven ground—the more surefooted my horses become. Trail riding supports the horse's overall training and suppleness.

EXERCISES OUT ON THE TRAIL

I also practice dressage movements when out riding, on slopes or in fields. This places new kinds of demands on the horses, but they tend not to notice the exertion as much because they are busy thinking about their surroundings, the ground beneath their hooves, and the horses in front of or behind them, when we are in a group. All these different stimuli help each horse become calm and well-balanced, and the environment gives his movements impulsion as if by magic.

LENGTHENED STRIDES

LENGTHENED STRIDES IN TROT

Riding lengthened strides improves the basic gaits. Energetically pushing off creates expressive, ground-covering movements. Lengthening the stride works better out on the trail than in an indoor or outdoor arena because the horse's movement already has more impulsion.

The rider must prepare to lengthen the trot stride using half-halts to gather the hindquarters underneath the horse and coil the horse's body like a spring. Forward leg aids in combination with an allowing hand create energy that is released in the form of ground-covering strides that are full of impulsion, but still controlled.

When lengthening the stride, make sure the horse's back is relaxed and his rhythm is maintained. As a rider, you will notice as soon as the horse tenses up, because you won't be able to sit the trot as easily. If that happens, I recommend riding the lengthened strides while posting, as this will activate the hindquarters more and take strain off the horse's back at the same time. Give it another quick try and bring the horse back. Then try sitting the lengthened trot again, and notice the difference.

Showing impulsion in lengthened trot strides in a field. (We inspected it for holes and tractor tire tracks first.)

An expressive return to a collected trot in good self-carriage.

Firlefranz shows off his impulsion at the trot in the snow.

The aim of lengthening the stride is to achieve medium or extended trot. The rider must make sure the horse steps evenly into the bridle and stays straight. The horse's stride lengthens when his hindquarters push more powerfully and his forehand moves more freely. The horse should remain in self-carriage while clearly lengthening his body, with his nose slightly before the vertical. The poll should still be the highest point.

Even snow doesn't stop dressage training. It gives horses an extra boost that I can make good use of for certain exercises. Like cavalletti training, work on slopes, or riding in water, riding in snow works and strengthens muscles in the whole body. But don't overdo it. Horses find moving in deep snow strenuous. You shouldn't ask too much of your horse, even if you are both having fun. Ride lengthened strides in short bursts, and don't forget to take the necessary breaks in walk to recover.

Freudentänzer: Springy trot strides in deep snow.

LENGTHENED STRIDES IN CANTER

If your horse is relaxed and in self-carriage in working canter, increase the pace over a short distance by lengthening his strides into medium canter. You are asking for longer, more ground-covering canter strides. The movement should be uphill, with the croup low rather than flat. This is normally achievable in a dressage seat, but your upper body shouldn't be too far back. However, you can also ride an active working canter and lengthened strides in a forward seat. From experience, I have found that you can ride bigger, more ground-covering movements in trot and especially in canter if you have the chance to incorporate loosening the horse up through lengthened strides in gallops outside the arena. Everything is easier and comes more naturally on the trail because the work is better suited to the horse's nature as an athletic animal.

Ground-covering canter in good self-carriage.

Franziskus does a good uphill flying change.

FLYING CHANGES

My young horses normally learn flying changes during their winter work between the ages of five and six. Learning flying changes is an important training goal for most horse sports, and I need to spend a lot of time on it. Some horses take a little longer to grasp the correct flying change, and I must be patient, careful, and precise when teaching it. I can only start playing with tempi changes once the single flying change is firmly established. Franziskus learned flying changes very quickly, and tempi changes are often a highlight of his dressage performances.

I only ride lead changes out on the trail when my horse has mastered them in the arena. Out on the trail, I can make use of the dynamic movement, increased ground coverage, and greater impulsion to improve the flying changes.

WORKING ON FLYING CHANGES

The canter must be collected enough, and the horse must respond promptly to subtle aids for a simple change before you can start trying flying changes. The easiest way to work on flying changes is as follows: In the arena, go onto a circle at A or C, and ride a figure eight so you are always riding the flying change over the centerline. I like to ride flying changes facing a mirror so I can see whether the horse is straight and whether his forehand and hindquarters are in line. I gradually reduce the number of walk strides in the lead change until I'm down to just one. The horse's canter must be collected, and he must canter on in response to subtle aids. Ideally, he should feel like he wants to go into canter again. I then leave out the walk stride and give the aid to change. To do so, I shift my weight onto my new inside seat bone, move my inside leg forward and my outside leg back, and give with my new inside hand to encourage the horse's new inside hind leg to step under.

Every time a change is successful, I come back to walk and praise the horse. I'd advise having somebody on the ground who can spot a correct change, so you praise the horse at the right time. When the change wasn't good, I just ride on and try again when the horse is responding well to my half-halts.

A late-season hay or crop field is a good places to practice lengthened canter strides.

SUPPLING — FLYING CHANGES

Straight and in good self-carriage.

changes one after the other too often, as this can make sensitive horses nervous. It's better to work on some other exercises to get the horse listening to the rider's aids again. Then go back to practicing the changes, this time somewhere else. With overeager horses, it can help to ride without spurs so you can use the flat of your calf more effectively. If you have a clever horse who anticipates the aids, it's important to give clear aids at the correct moment to get the timing right. I also like to ride flying changes without stirrups from time to time because it enables me to drive with my seat and use the flat of my calf more effectively.

If the horse becomes tense after the change, I can either relieve the tension with some lengthened strides on a straightaway or come back to walk and praise the horse.

FLYING CHANGES OUT ON THE TRAIL

Here's another option for working on flying changes: Start by riding a few simple changes on a circle, such that you change into counter-canter on the open side and into true canter on the closed side. You should only really need one stride of walk for the change. Always ride the change in the same place to make it easier for the horse to understand the exercise. After a few simple changes, leave out the walk stride and try a flying change from counter-canter into true canter. You need to activate the hindquarters, collect the horse, and give the aids for the change clearly.

When teaching a horse flying changes, it's sometimes advisable not to ride the

As the horse is learning the flying changes, I must give the aids more clearly; only later on will they gradually become invisible. A change can only be as good as the collected canter that comes before it. Once a horse has mastered the flying change, he needs to learn to wait for the aids for the change and not anticipate. That's why I ride changes in different places and on different lines, including on the trail. The horse's canter should be collected, uphill, in front of the aids, and in an even rhythm.

A relaxing stroll through the countryside is a good way to finish.

In between the individual changes, I need to keep cantering forward and releasing the horse's impulsion at the right time to maintain the quality of his canter. Out on the trail, I make use of natural paths and always ride clean flying changes before a bend in the trail. This is a fun way for horses to learn, and it mimics what they would do in the wild without a rider. When you manage a good change, end your training session there. I like to stop on a good note before practicing again the next day or the day after. It's especially important to let the horse have a good stretch in canter after this exercise. I then come back to rising trot and let the horse stretch all the way down, until my reins are at the buckle. He should still be moving forward actively. I come back to walk and give the horse lots of praise.

FINISH AT THE RIGHT TIME

For training to be successful, it's important to notice when your horse is starting to max out his strength and stamina. When riding out on the trail, remember that the horse's increased desire for forward movement can sometimes conceal diminishing energy. Know when to stop.

DRESSAGE OUTSIDE THE "SANDBOX"

Freudentänzer canters springily on a light contact.

Franziskus shows his expressive, dynamic trot.

Photo Feature — Dressage Outside the "Sandbox"

Motivated and focused, Franziskus does flying changes in a field.

Dresden Mann in piaffe.

A snack as a reward!

USEFUL INFORMATION
—last but not least

FURTHER READING

Baumert, Beth: *When Two Spines Align: Dressage Dynamics.* Trafalgar Square Books, 2014.

How do we make two different bodies move in absolute harmony? This book provides the key to better riding, and explains how to develop balance as a rider and refine your feel and timing. Learn to direct and shape your horse's energy.

Baumert, Beth: *How Two Minds Meet: The Mental Dynamics of Dressage.* Trafalgar Square Books, 2020.

Ideally, when riding, not only do two bodies move in harmony, but two mental systems also work in harmony. The horse opens up both physically and mentally. This is shown by accepting the rider's aids and carrying out the lessons correctly—sometimes with the rider just thinking about them. In this book, Beth Baumert describes how every rider can achieve this mental connection.

Gösmeier, Dr. med. vet. Ina: *The 5 Horse Types: Traditional Chinese Medicine for Training and Caring for Every Horse.* Trafalgar Square Books, 2020.

From the perspective of traditional Chinese medicine, illnesses or behavioral disorders always have a physical and a mental aspect. Physical and psychological problems are related to each other. Traditional Chinese medicine therefore always treats holistically. In this guide, the renowned veterinarian Dr. Ina Gösmeier describes the five types of horses and their individual treatment. Extra: TCM herbal recipes, acupressure and many case studies.

Jones, Janet: *Horse Brain, Human Brain: The Neuroscience of Horsemanship.* Trafalgar Square Books, 2020.

The brain controls behavior—in horses as well as in humans. The neuroscientist and successful trainer Janet Jones explains the similarities and differences between the brains of humans and horses in an easy-to-understand manner and shows how to apply this knowledge to make education, training, and handling efficient and solution-oriented.

Klimke, Ingrid / Klimke, Reiner: *Cavalletti for Dressage and Jumping.* Trafalgar Square Books, 2018.

An important cornerstone of Ingrid Klimke's success is cavalletti work. This guide shows cavalletti work on the lunge, and provides valuable new suggestions for dressage work as well as numerous updated diagrams and arena tracks for jumping gymnastics. In addition to the exercise of the horse and the associated improvement of gait, cavalletti work brings fun and variety to everyday training..

Klimke, Ingrid / Klimke, Reiner: *Basic Training of the Young Horse: Dressage—Jumping—Cross-Country.* Trafalgar Square Books, 2019.

The name "Klimke" stands for horse-friendly and versatile training. The first months and years under saddle lay the foundation for the future of a riding horse. Every horse, whether used in sport or ridden for leisure, needs solid and well-founded basic training so he can carry out his tasks under the rider reliably, with motivation, and in the best possible health. No book describes the basic training of young riding horses as thoroughly as this classic.

Klimke, Ingrid: *Training Horses the Ingrid Klimke Way: An Olympic Medalist's Winning Methods for a Joyful Riding Partnership.* Trafalgar Square Books, 2017.

With Ingrid Klimke, horses and people enjoy training. The core points of her horse-friendly training philosophy are cavalletti work, dressage, jumping and riding in the field. Using her own horses as an example, she gives valuable tips on how to promote each horse's character.

Nölke, Marc: *Neuroathletics for Riders: Innovative Exercises That Train Your Brain and Change Your Nervous System for Optimal Health and Peak Performance.* Trafalgar Square Books, 2023.

With this book, you will become a better rider without having to practice riding—because neuroathletics improves riding technique through exercises for the brain. The method of the successful trainer Mark Nölke specifically trains those areas of the brain that are responsible for stability, sense of rhythm, and movement precision, as well as the visual center. This improves mobility and posture, solves muscle problems, strengthens the ability to concentrate, and even overcomes fears and trauma.